Copyright © 2023 by Herman Strange (Author)

All rights reserved. This book or any portion thereof may not be reproduced or used in any manner whatsoever without the express written permission of the publisher except for the use of brief quotations in a book review.

This book is copyright protected. This is only for personal use. You cannot amend, distributor, sell, use, quote or paraphrase any part or the content within this book without the consent of the author. Please note the information contained within this document is for educational and entertainment purposes only. Every attempt has been made to provide accurate, up to date and reliable complete information. No warranties of any kind are expressed or implied.

Readers acknowledge that the author is not engaging in the rendering of legal, financial, medical or professional advice. The content of this book has been derived from various sources. Please consult a licensed professional before attempting any techniques outlined in this book.

By reading this document, the readers agree that under no circumstances are the author responsible for any losses, direct or indirect, which are incurred as a result of the use of information contained within this document, including but not limited to errors, omissions or inaccuracies.

Thank you very much for reading this book.

Title: Social Connecting for Health-The Importance of Relationships for Overall Wellness
Subtitle: The Role of Social Connections in Building Resilience

Series: Healthy Habits for Life: Building Sustainable Habits for Optimal Health and Wellness
Author: Serenity Tanner

Table of Contents

Introduction 5
Importance of Maintaining Social Connections 5
Purpose of the Book 8
Overview of Social Connections and Their Benefits 11

Chapter 1: Types of Social Connections 14
Description of Different Types of Connections 14
Health Benefits of Each Type 19
Examples of Each Type 22

Chapter 2: Technology for Social Connections 27
Latest Technology for Staying Connected 27
Pros and Cons 30
Popular Brands and Devices 33

Chapter 3: Building and Maintaining Social Connections 37
Tips and Tricks for Building and Maintaining Connections 37
Activities and Hobbies to Connect with Others 40
Overcoming Barriers to Connection 43

Chapter 4: Social Connections and Mental Health 46
Importance of Social Connections for Mental Health 46
Common Mental Health Challenges and How to Address Them 48
How Social Connections Can Help with Mental Health . 52

Chapter 5: Comparing and Contrasting Methods .. 54
Summary of Pros and Cons..54
Criteria for Comparison..58
Recommendations for Different Needs........................... 61
Conclusion 63
Recap of Importance of Maintaining Social Connections
..63
Final Thoughts and Recommendations........................... 65
Potential References... 67

Introduction
Importance of Maintaining Social Connections

In today's digital age, we are more connected than ever before. Social media, messaging apps, and video conferencing platforms have made it easier than ever to stay in touch with family, friends, and even strangers from around the world. However, despite this increased connectivity, studies show that rates of loneliness and social isolation are on the rise. In fact, some experts have described this as a "loneliness epidemic" that is having a profound impact on our physical and mental health.

The purpose of this book is to explore the importance of social connections for our health and well-being. In this chapter, we will discuss the reasons why social connections are so crucial, as well as the risks associated with social isolation.

Social connections are an essential aspect of human life. From the moment we are born, we rely on social interactions to develop our communication skills, emotional regulation, and sense of self. As we grow older, social connections continue to play a critical role in our lives. They provide us with a sense of belonging, purpose, and meaning.

At a basic level, social connections help us meet our fundamental human needs. Humans are social creatures, and we require a sense of connection to others in order to thrive. When we are surrounded by positive social interactions, our brains release chemicals like oxytocin and dopamine, which can help us feel happy, secure, and fulfilled. On the other hand, when we are socially isolated, our brains release stress hormones like cortisol, which can have a detrimental impact on our physical and mental health.

In addition to meeting our basic needs, social connections also provide a number of specific health benefits. Studies show that people with strong social connections are at a lower risk of developing a wide range of health problems, including depression, anxiety, cardiovascular disease, and even dementia. Social connections can also help us manage chronic conditions like diabetes or cancer, by providing us with emotional support and practical assistance when we need it.

Despite the clear benefits of social connections, many of us struggle to maintain these connections in our busy, technology-focused lives. We may feel too busy or overwhelmed to make time for social activities, or we may struggle to connect with others due to cultural or social barriers. In some cases, we may even be actively avoiding social connections due to fears or negative experiences.

In order to combat these challenges, it is essential that we understand the importance of social connections and make a conscious effort to prioritize them in our lives. Whether we are connecting with family members, friends, or community members, social connections are a vital aspect of our overall health and well-being. In the following chapters, we will explore different types of social connections, strategies for building and maintaining these connections, and the impact of social connections on our mental health.

Purpose of the Book

The purpose of this book is to provide readers with a comprehensive guide to staying connected in a digital age. In this chapter, we will discuss the specific goals of this book, as well as the audience we hope to reach.

The primary purpose of this book is to provide readers with a practical guide to building and maintaining social connections in a digital age. We will explore the different types of social connections that exist, including familial, romantic, and platonic relationships. We will also provide strategies for building and maintaining these connections, including tips for overcoming common barriers to connection.

One of the key goals of this book is to help readers understand the impact of social connections on their health and well-being. We will explore the specific health benefits of social connections, including their impact on mental health, physical health, and even mortality rates. By understanding the importance of social connections, we hope to motivate readers to prioritize connection in their own lives.

In addition to discussing the benefits of social connections, we will also explore the potential risks associated with social isolation. We will discuss the negative impact that loneliness can have on our physical and mental health, as well as the role that technology can play in exacerbating feelings of isolation.

Another goal of this book is to provide readers with practical strategies for using technology to stay connected with others. We will explore the latest technology for staying connected, including popular brands and devices. We will also discuss the pros and cons of using technology for social connections, and provide tips for using technology in a healthy and balanced way.

Finally, we hope to provide readers with a framework for understanding and comparing different methods of social connection. We will discuss the pros and cons of different types of social connections, as well as the specific criteria that readers should consider when choosing a method of connection. By providing readers with a comprehensive overview of different methods of social connection, we hope to help them make informed decisions about how to stay connected with others.

Audience:

This book is intended for anyone who is interested in staying connected with others in a digital age. This may include individuals who are struggling with social isolation or loneliness, as well as those who are interested in improving their overall health and well-being. We hope that this book will be accessible to readers from a wide range of backgrounds and experiences, and that it will provide practical tips and strategies that readers can apply to their own lives.

Overview of Social Connections and Their Benefits

Social connections are an essential part of the human experience. From early childhood to late adulthood, social connections play a critical role in our physical and mental health, as well as our overall quality of life. In this chapter, we will provide an overview of social connections and their benefits, including the specific ways in which social connections can impact our health and well-being.

Social connections can take many forms, including familial relationships, friendships, romantic relationships, and community connections. These connections can be nurtured and maintained over time, or they can be disrupted or lost due to a variety of factors.

Research has shown that social connections play a vital role in our physical health. Studies have found that individuals with strong social connections are more likely to live longer, experience less chronic illness, and recover more quickly from illness or injury. This may be due in part to the fact that social connections can provide us with emotional support, which can help to reduce stress and promote better overall health.

Social connections are also critical to our mental health. Studies have shown that individuals with strong social connections are less likely to experience depression, anxiety, and other mental health disorders. They are also more likely to have higher self-esteem, greater feelings of happiness and life satisfaction, and better coping skills for dealing with stress and adversity.

Beyond the specific benefits to physical and mental health, social connections are also essential for our overall quality of life. Social connections can provide us with a sense of belonging and purpose, as well as opportunities for personal growth and development. They can also help us to feel more connected to our communities, and to have a sense of meaning and purpose in our lives.

Benefits of Different Types of Social Connections:

Different types of social connections can provide unique benefits to our health and well-being. For example, research has shown that strong familial relationships can provide a sense of stability and support that can help to promote better mental and physical health. Romantic relationships can provide a sense of intimacy and connection that can help to promote feelings of happiness and life satisfaction. Friendships can provide a sense of camaraderie and shared experiences that can help to promote a sense of belonging and purpose.

Community connections can also be critical to our health and well-being. These connections can include participation in civic organizations, volunteering, or simply spending time with neighbors or friends in our local communities. Community connections can provide a sense of belonging and purpose, as well as opportunities for personal growth and development. They can also help to promote greater social cohesion, and a sense of shared purpose and identity.

In conclusion, social connections are an essential part of the human experience. They play a critical role in our physical and mental health, as well as our overall quality of life. By understanding the specific benefits of social connections, and the ways in which they can impact our health and well-being, we can be more intentional about building and maintaining connections in our own lives.

Chapter 1: Types of Social Connections
Description of Different Types of Connections

Social connections can take many forms, each with its own unique benefits and challenges. In this chapter, we will explore the different types of social connections, including familial relationships, friendships, romantic relationships, and community connections. We will also discuss the benefits of each type of connection, as well as some of the challenges that can arise when maintaining these connections.

Familial Relationships:

Familial relationships refer to the connections we have with our family members, including parents, siblings, grandparents, and other relatives. These relationships can be some of the most important connections we have, providing a sense of belonging and stability throughout our lives.

Familial relationships can take many forms, from close-knit families who spend a lot of time together, to more distant relationships where family members may only see each other occasionally. Regardless of the specific dynamics of the relationship, familial connections can provide a sense of history and shared experience, which can be important for maintaining a sense of identity and purpose.

At the same time, familial relationships can also be some of the most challenging to maintain. Family dynamics can be complex, and disagreements and conflicts can arise that make it difficult to maintain strong connections. Additionally, family members may live far away from each other or have different lifestyles, which can make it challenging to stay connected over time.

Friendships:

Friendships are another important type of social connection. These relationships can provide a sense of camaraderie and shared experiences, which can be important for promoting a sense of belonging and purpose. Friendships can take many forms, from close friendships with people we see frequently, to more distant relationships where we may only see our friends occasionally.

The benefits of friendships are numerous. Friends can provide emotional support during difficult times, and can help to promote feelings of happiness and well-being. Additionally, friends can help us to build social skills and confidence, and can provide opportunities for personal growth and development.

At the same time, maintaining friendships can be challenging. As we get older and our lives become more complex, it can be difficult to find time to spend with friends.

Additionally, conflicts and disagreements can arise in friendships, which can make it difficult to maintain strong connections over time.

Romantic Relationships:

Romantic relationships are another important type of social connection. These relationships can provide a sense of intimacy and connection that is difficult to find in other types of relationships. Romantic relationships can take many forms, from casual dating to long-term committed relationships.

The benefits of romantic relationships are numerous. Romantic partners can provide emotional support during difficult times, and can help to promote feelings of happiness and well-being. Additionally, romantic relationships can provide a sense of purpose and meaning, and can be an important source of personal growth and development.

At the same time, maintaining a romantic relationship can be challenging. Conflicts and disagreements can arise, and partners may have different needs and expectations that can be difficult to navigate. Additionally, as relationships become more serious, issues around commitment and long-term compatibility can arise.

Community Connections:

Community connections refer to the connections we have with our local communities, including neighbors, colleagues, and other community members. These relationships can provide a sense of belonging and purpose, as well as opportunities for personal growth and development.

Community connections can take many forms, from participating in civic organizations to volunteering in local charities or community events. The benefits of community connections are numerous. They can help to promote social cohesion and a sense of shared identity, and can provide opportunities for personal growth and development.

At the same time, maintaining community connections can be challenging. It can be difficult to find time to participate in community events, and conflicts and disagreements can arise with other community members. Additionally, as communities change over time, it can be difficult to maintain a sense of connection and belonging.

In conclusion, it is clear that social connections play a vital role in our overall health and well-being. Maintaining social connections is not just a matter of preference or convenience, but a necessity for our physical, emotional, and mental health. As we have seen in this book, social connections come in many different forms, from family and friends to community organizations and online networks.

Understanding the different types of social connections and their unique benefits can help us make informed decisions about how we choose to stay connected. By utilizing the latest technology and implementing strategies to build and maintain social connections, we can improve our health and quality of life.

It is my hope that this book has provided valuable insights into the importance of social connections and practical tips for staying connected. By following the guidance presented here, we can all take steps to create a more connected and fulfilling life. Remember, social connections are the key to staying healthy and happy, so let's make them a priority in our lives.

Health Benefits of Each Type

There are many different types of social connections, and each type provides unique health benefits. In this chapter, we will explore the different types of social connections and how they contribute to our overall health and well-being.

1. Family Connections Family connections are the social connections we have with our immediate family, including parents, siblings, and children. These connections provide us with a sense of belonging, identity, and purpose. Family connections also give us a support system to help us through difficult times, such as illness or loss.

Research has shown that strong family connections are associated with better mental health outcomes, including reduced risk of depression and anxiety. Family connections also contribute to physical health, such as reduced risk of cardiovascular disease, improved immune function, and increased longevity.

2. Friendships Friendships are social connections we have with people outside our family who we share common interests, experiences, or values with. Friendships can provide emotional support, companionship, and a sense of belonging.

Studies have shown that having close friendships is associated with lower levels of stress, improved mental health outcomes, and increased self-esteem. Friendships also contribute to physical health, such as reduced risk of chronic diseases and increased longevity.

3. Romantic Relationships Romantic relationships are social connections we have with our partners. These connections can provide emotional support, companionship, and a sense of intimacy.

Research has shown that healthy romantic relationships are associated with better mental health outcomes, including reduced risk of depression and anxiety. They also contribute to physical health, such as lower levels of stress and improved immune function.

4. Community Connections Community connections are social connections we have with our neighbors, local organizations, and other community members. These connections provide a sense of belonging, identity, and purpose. Community connections also provide opportunities for social engagement and support.

Studies have shown that strong community connections are associated with better mental health outcomes, including reduced risk of depression and anxiety.

They also contribute to physical health, such as reduced risk of chronic diseases and increased longevity.

5. Online Connections Online connections are social connections we have through social media platforms, online forums, and other digital channels. These connections provide a sense of belonging and support, as well as opportunities for social engagement and collaboration.

Research has shown that online connections can be beneficial for mental health, particularly for people who are socially isolated or have difficulty connecting with others in person. However, there are also potential negative consequences of online connections, such as cyberbullying and social media addiction.

In conclusion, each type of social connection provides unique health benefits. By understanding the different types of social connections and their associated benefits, we can make informed decisions about how to stay connected with others and improve our overall health and well-being.

Examples of Each Type

In this chapter, we have explored the different types of social connections and the health benefits they provide. Now, let's take a closer look at some examples of each type of social connection.

1. Family Connections Family connections are the social connections we have with our immediate family, including parents, siblings, and children. Here are some examples of family connections:

- Parent-child relationships: This can include relationships between parents and their young children, as well as adult children and their aging parents. These relationships often involve emotional support, guidance, and shared experiences.

- Sibling relationships: Siblings share a unique bond that can last a lifetime. Sibling relationships can involve emotional support, shared experiences, and even conflict.

- Extended family relationships: This can include relationships with grandparents, aunts, uncles, and cousins. These relationships can provide a sense of belonging and support, as well as opportunities for family gatherings and traditions.

2. Friendships Friendships are social connections we have with people outside our family who we share common

interests, experiences, or values with. Here are some examples of friendships:

- Childhood friends: These are friends we have known since childhood and have grown up with. Childhood friends can provide emotional support, shared experiences, and a sense of belonging.

- Work friends: These are friends we have made through our jobs or careers. Work friends can provide emotional support, as well as opportunities for collaboration and networking.

- Online friends: These are friends we have made through social media or other online platforms. Online friends can provide emotional support and opportunities for social engagement.

3. Romantic Relationships Romantic relationships are social connections we have with our partners. Here are some examples of romantic relationships:

- Dating relationships: These are relationships that involve going on dates and spending time together. Dating relationships can provide emotional support, companionship, and a sense of intimacy.

- Long-term relationships: These are relationships that have lasted for several years and often involve living together or getting married. Long-term relationships can provide emotional support, stability, and a sense of shared identity.

- Same-sex relationships: These are romantic relationships between people of the same gender. Same-sex relationships can provide emotional support, companionship, and a sense of belonging to a larger community.

4. Community Connections Community connections are social connections we have with our neighbors, local organizations, and other community members. Here are some examples of community connections:

- Neighborhood relationships: These are relationships with people who live in our local communities. Neighborhood relationships can provide a sense of belonging, support, and opportunities for social engagement.

- Volunteer relationships: These are relationships we have with people we volunteer with for a particular cause or organization. Volunteer relationships can provide a sense of shared purpose and opportunities for collaboration.

- Religious relationships: These are relationships we have with members of our religious communities. Religious relationships can provide a sense of belonging, emotional support, and shared values.

5. Online Connections Online connections are social connections we have through social media platforms, online forums, and other digital channels. Here are some examples of online connections:

- Social media connections: These are connections we have with people through social media platforms such as Facebook, Twitter, or Instagram. Social media connections can provide a sense of belonging and support, as well as opportunities for social engagement and collaboration.

- Online community connections: These are connections we have with people through online forums or communities based on shared interests or hobbies. Online community connections can provide a sense of belonging and support, as well as opportunities for social engagement.

- Virtual relationships: These are relationships we have with people we have never met in person, such as through online gaming or chat rooms. Virtual relationships can provide a sense of belonging and support, as well as opportunities for social engagement and collaboration.

In conclusion, each type of social connection provides unique opportunities for individuals to fulfill their social needs and reap various health benefits. Maintaining a diverse range of social connections can contribute to a sense of belonging, purpose, and overall well-being. Family connections provide a foundation of support and unconditional love, while friendships can offer companionship and a source of fun and enjoyment. Community connections allow individuals to feel connected to a larger social network and can promote a sense of civic responsibility. Professional connections can offer career opportunities and mentorship, while romantic connections can provide emotional intimacy and support. By understanding the different types of social connections available and the benefits they provide, individuals can make intentional efforts to prioritize and strengthen their relationships, leading to a happier and healthier life.

Chapter 2: Technology for Social Connections
Latest Technology for Staying Connected

Technology has revolutionized the way we connect with others, making it easier than ever to stay in touch and maintain relationships. In this chapter, we will explore the latest technology for staying connected and how it can benefit our social lives.

One of the most popular forms of technology for social connections is social media. Social media platforms like Facebook, Twitter, and Instagram allow users to connect with friends and family, share photos and updates, and engage in discussions and conversations. Social media can be particularly beneficial for maintaining long-distance relationships and keeping in touch with those we might not see regularly.

Another popular technology for social connections is messaging apps. Messaging apps like WhatsApp, Telegram, and WeChat allow users to send instant messages, voice notes, and even make voice or video calls. These apps are particularly useful for connecting with friends and family across different time zones or for group chats and discussions.

Video conferencing technology has also become increasingly popular, particularly in light of the COVID-19 pandemic. Platforms like Zoom, Skype, and Google Meet allow users to connect face-to-face from the comfort of their own homes. Video conferencing can be particularly beneficial for maintaining professional connections or for connecting with friends and family who are unable to meet in person.

In recent years, virtual reality (VR) and augmented reality (AR) technology have also emerged as new ways to connect with others. VR and AR technologies allow users to enter virtual spaces and interact with others in a simulated environment. This technology has the potential to revolutionize the way we connect with others, particularly for those who are unable to travel or participate in real-life events.

Finally, wearable technology like smartwatches and fitness trackers can also facilitate social connections. Many of these devices include social features like messaging and call notifications, as well as health and fitness tracking capabilities that can encourage group fitness activities or competitions.

Overall, the latest technology for staying connected offers a diverse range of opportunities for individuals to connect with others and maintain relationships. By embracing these technologies, individuals can stay connected with loved ones, engage in new social experiences, and lead happier and healthier lives.

Pros and Cons

While technology has greatly improved our ability to connect with others, it's important to recognize both the benefits and drawbacks of using these tools for social connections. In this section, we'll examine the pros and cons of technology for social connections.

Pros:

1. Convenience: One of the biggest advantages of technology is that it makes it easy and convenient to stay in touch with others, regardless of location or time. With social media and messaging apps, we can connect with friends and family members from anywhere in the world, at any time of day.

2. Greater social opportunities: Technology also offers greater social opportunities, allowing us to connect with people we might not otherwise have had the chance to meet. Social media, for example, can connect us with individuals who share our interests, while video conferencing can allow us to connect with colleagues or clients from different parts of the world.

3. Improved mental health: Staying connected with others can have positive effects on our mental health, and technology can help make that easier. For individuals who may have trouble leaving the house or who experience social

anxiety, technology provides a low-pressure way to connect with others and maintain social relationships.

4. Enhanced learning opportunities: Technology can also provide opportunities for learning and personal growth. Social media can offer insights into different cultures or help individuals learn about new ideas, while video conferencing can facilitate educational opportunities, such as language learning.

Cons:

1. Overuse: One of the biggest drawbacks of technology for social connections is the risk of overuse. Constantly checking social media or responding to messages can lead to a loss of productivity or the neglect of other important areas of life.

2. Decreased face-to-face interaction: Technology can also decrease the amount of face-to-face interaction that we have with others, which can have negative effects on social skills and relationship-building abilities.

3. Cyberbullying: Cyberbullying is a major risk associated with technology, particularly for young people. It's important to use social media and messaging apps safely and to educate children about the potential risks associated with online interactions.

4. Decreased privacy: Finally, technology for social connections can also have negative effects on privacy, with many apps and platforms collecting personal data and potentially sharing it with third parties.

In conclusion, while technology for social connections has many benefits, it's important to be aware of the potential drawbacks and risks associated with its use. By using technology mindfully and safely, individuals can enjoy the benefits of staying connected while mitigating the potential negative effects.

Popular Brands and Devices

Social connections have become increasingly important in a digital age, and technology has played a significant role in facilitating these connections. With the rise of social media, video conferencing, and other digital platforms, people can now connect with others from anywhere in the world. In this chapter, we will explore the latest technology for staying connected, including the most popular brands and devices.

Popular Brands

1. Facebook: Facebook is one of the most popular social media platforms, with over 2.7 billion active users worldwide. The platform allows users to connect with family and friends, join groups, and share photos and videos.

2. Instagram: Instagram is a photo and video-sharing app that has over 1 billion active users. The app is popular among young people and allows users to connect with others, follow influencers and brands, and share their own content.

3. Twitter: Twitter is a microblogging platform with over 330 million active users. The platform allows users to share short messages, or "tweets," with their followers, making it a great platform for sharing news, opinions, and updates.

4. TikTok: TikTok is a video-sharing app that has become increasingly popular in recent years, particularly among younger users. The app allows users to create short videos set to music and share them with their followers.

5. LinkedIn: LinkedIn is a social media platform designed for professionals. With over 700 million active users, LinkedIn allows users to connect with other professionals in their industry, share their experience and expertise, and search for job opportunities.

Popular Devices

1. Smartphones: Smartphones are the most popular devices for staying connected. With the ability to make calls, send texts, and access social media and other digital platforms, smartphones allow people to stay connected on-the-go.

2. Laptops: Laptops are a popular device for staying connected, particularly for work-related activities. With the ability to access email, video conferencing platforms, and other digital tools, laptops allow people to stay connected with colleagues and clients from anywhere.

3. Tablets: Tablets are a lightweight and portable option for staying connected. With a larger screen than a smartphone and more portability than a laptop, tablets are a

great option for consuming content, browsing social media, and video chatting.

4. Smartwatches: Smartwatches are a newer technology that allows people to stay connected without needing to take out their smartphone. With the ability to make calls, send texts, and access apps, smartwatches are a convenient way to stay connected on-the-go.

Pros and Cons

While technology has made it easier to stay connected, there are both pros and cons to using digital platforms for social connections. Here are some of the main pros and cons:

Pros:

1. Increased connectivity: Technology has made it easier to connect with people from all over the world, and has made it easier to maintain long-distance relationships.

2. Convenience: Digital platforms make it easy to stay connected on-the-go, and allow people to connect with others at any time.

3. Greater sense of community: Social media and other digital platforms allow people to connect with others who share their interests and values, creating a greater sense of community.

Cons:

1. Decreased face-to-face interaction: The use of technology for social connections can lead to decreased face-to-face interaction, which can lead to feelings of isolation and loneliness.

2. Cyberbullying: Cyberbullying is a growing problem on social media platforms, and can lead to negative mental health effects.

3. Addiction: The use of digital platforms can be addictive, leading to a decrease in productivity and a negative impact on mental health.

Overall, while technology has made it easier to stay connected, it's important to be aware of the potential downsides and to use technology in a way that enhances, rather than hinders, our social connections. By understanding the pros and cons of different devices and platforms, we can make informed decisions about how we use technology to connect with others. It's also important to remember that technology is just one tool for staying connected, and that in-person connections are still crucial for our overall well-being. With a balanced approach to technology and a variety of social connections, we can reap the many benefits of social connectedness in the digital age.

Chapter 3: Building and Maintaining Social Connections
Tips and Tricks for Building and Maintaining Connections

Building and maintaining social connections is essential for our mental, emotional, and physical well-being. Here are some tips and tricks for establishing and nurturing social connections:

1. Be proactive: Take the initiative to reach out to others and make plans. Whether it's inviting a colleague to lunch, setting up a virtual game night with friends, or joining a local club or group, making the effort to connect with others is crucial.

2. Show interest: When interacting with others, show genuine interest in what they have to say. Ask questions, listen actively, and validate their feelings. This helps build trust and fosters deeper connections.

3. Practice gratitude: Take time to appreciate the people in your life and express gratitude for their presence. This can be as simple as sending a thank-you note or telling someone how much they mean to you.

4. Use social media mindfully: Social media can be a powerful tool for staying connected, but it can also lead to feelings of loneliness and isolation. Use social media

mindfully, setting boundaries around how much time you spend on it and how you engage with others online.

5. Pursue common interests: Find people who share your interests and engage in activities together. This can help you build a sense of community and foster a sense of belonging.

6. Volunteer: Volunteering for a cause you care about can provide opportunities to meet new people and build connections with others who share your values and passions.

7. Be open-minded: Be open to meeting new people and forming connections with those who may be different from you. Embracing diversity can enrich your life and broaden your perspective.

8. Practice active listening: When engaging in conversation, practice active listening by being fully present and focused on the speaker. Avoid distractions and show interest in what they have to say.

9. Join a support group: If you're dealing with a challenging situation, consider joining a support group where you can connect with others who are going through similar experiences.

10. Seek professional help: If you're struggling to build and maintain social connections, consider seeking professional help. A mental health professional can provide

guidance and support as you work to strengthen your social connections.

By implementing these tips and tricks, you can establish and nurture meaningful social connections that can enhance your overall well-being.

Activities and Hobbies to Connect with Others

Engaging in activities and hobbies is an excellent way to build and maintain social connections. Participating in activities that you enjoy with like-minded individuals can lead to the development of friendships and can help to create a sense of community. Here are some activities and hobbies that you can explore to help you connect with others:

1. Join a Club or Group: Joining a club or group is an excellent way to meet new people who share your interests. There are many different types of groups and clubs that you can join, such as book clubs, sports clubs, or hobby groups. Look for groups that meet regularly and have a schedule of activities that you can participate in.

2. Volunteer: Volunteering is an excellent way to meet new people and to give back to your community. You can volunteer for local charities, non-profit organizations, or community groups. Volunteering can also help to give you a sense of purpose and can lead to personal growth.

3. Attend Community Events: Attending community events is an excellent way to meet new people and to connect with others in your community. Look for events such as street fairs, farmers markets, or local festivals. These events often have a festive atmosphere, making it easier to strike up a conversation with someone new.

4. Take a Class: Taking a class is an excellent way to learn something new and to meet new people who share your interests. Look for classes at your local community center or adult education program. You can take classes in anything from cooking to dance to art.

5. Join a Sports Team: Joining a sports team is an excellent way to meet new people and to get some exercise. Look for local sports leagues or pick-up games in your area. Joining a sports team can also help to build teamwork skills and can lead to personal growth.

6. Attend Meetup Events: Meetup is an online platform that allows people to organize and attend events with others who share their interests. Look for local Meetup groups that are focused on your interests, and attend the events that they organize.

7. Host a Dinner Party: Hosting a dinner party is an excellent way to bring people together and to connect with others in a more intimate setting. You can invite friends, family, and colleagues over for a meal, and use it as an opportunity to catch up and connect with one another.

8. Travel: Traveling is an excellent way to meet new people and to experience new cultures. Consider taking a solo trip or joining a group tour to meet like-minded individuals who share your interests.

In summary, participating in activities and hobbies is an excellent way to build and maintain social connections. By engaging in activities that you enjoy with like-minded individuals, you can develop friendships and create a sense of community. There are many different types of activities and hobbies that you can explore, from joining a club or group to attending community events or taking a class. By finding the right activities and hobbies that resonate with you, you can open yourself up to new social connections and experiences.

Overcoming Barriers to Connection

Building and maintaining social connections is important for our well-being and happiness, but it can be challenging. There are various barriers that can make it difficult to establish and maintain connections with others, including:

1. Time constraints: In our busy lives, we may struggle to find time to connect with others.

2. Shyness or social anxiety: For some people, initiating and sustaining social interactions can be intimidating and uncomfortable.

3. Geographic distance: We may be physically separated from the people we want to connect with due to distance or relocation.

4. Differences in lifestyle or interests: Sometimes, we may feel like we don't have much in common with the people around us, making it challenging to establish connections.

5. Language barriers: For those who speak a different language, it can be difficult to connect with others who don't speak the same language.

Fortunately, there are strategies we can use to overcome these barriers and establish meaningful social connections:

1. Prioritize social connections: Making social connections a priority is essential. This means carving out time in our busy schedules to connect with others and being intentional about building and maintaining those relationships.

2. Practice social skills: For those who struggle with social interactions, practicing social skills can be helpful. This might involve seeking out social situations and gradually building up comfort and confidence over time.

3. Use technology: While face-to-face interactions are ideal, technology can be a helpful tool for staying connected with others, particularly for those who are geographically distant. This might involve using video conferencing tools, social media platforms, or instant messaging apps.

4. Seek out common ground: When we feel like we don't have much in common with others, it can be helpful to seek out shared interests or activities. Joining a club or group focused on a shared hobby or interest can be a great way to connect with others who have similar passions.

5. Learn a new language: For those who speak a different language, learning the local language can be a great way to connect with others in the community. It can also be an opportunity to learn more about the local culture and customs.

6. Challenge negative thinking: Negative thinking patterns, such as assuming that others won't like us, can hold us back from connecting with others. Challenging these thoughts and replacing them with more positive and realistic thinking can help us to take risks and put ourselves out there.

By using these strategies, we can overcome the barriers to connection and establish meaningful social connections with others.

Chapter 4: Social Connections and Mental Health
Importance of Social Connections for Mental Health

Social connections are an essential aspect of mental health and well-being. Human beings are social animals and have a fundamental need to connect with others. When people feel connected and supported, they are more likely to experience positive emotions and have a sense of purpose in their lives. Conversely, a lack of social connection and support can lead to negative feelings such as loneliness, isolation, and despair.

Research has consistently shown that social connections are critical to mental health. People with strong social support networks are less likely to experience depression, anxiety, and other mental health problems. A study by the American Psychological Association found that social isolation and loneliness were associated with a higher risk of mental health problems, including depression and anxiety.

Social connections can also improve the outcomes of existing mental health problems. For example, individuals with depression who have strong social support networks may experience faster recovery times and are less likely to experience future depressive episodes.

The benefits of social connections for mental health can be explained by various factors. First, social connections provide emotional support, which helps individuals manage stress and cope with challenging situations. Second, social connections can increase feelings of self-worth and self-esteem, which can be protective against mental health problems. Third, social connections can provide a sense of belonging and purpose, which can improve overall well-being.

In summary, social connections are essential for maintaining good mental health. Individuals who feel connected and supported by others are less likely to experience mental health problems and can recover faster from existing problems. Given the crucial role that social connections play in mental health, it is essential to prioritize building and maintaining social relationships as part of a healthy lifestyle.

Common Mental Health Challenges and How to Address Them

In the modern world, mental health has become a major concern, with many people suffering from various mental health issues such as anxiety, depression, and stress. However, research has shown that social connections play a critical role in mental health and can even help to prevent and manage mental health conditions. In this section, we will explore the importance of social connections for mental health.

One of the main benefits of social connections is that they provide a sense of belonging and support. Having a strong support network of family, friends, and other social connections can help to reduce feelings of loneliness and isolation, which are known risk factors for mental health problems. Social connections can also provide emotional support and a safe space to share thoughts and feelings, which can help to alleviate stress and anxiety.

In addition, social connections can help to increase self-esteem and confidence, which are important factors in mental health. When we have positive social interactions, we feel valued and appreciated, which can boost our self-esteem and improve our mental well-being. Social connections can also provide opportunities for personal growth and development, which can help to build confidence and resilience.

*****

While social connections can have a positive impact on mental health, there are still many challenges that people face in maintaining and building these connections. In this section, we will explore some of the common mental health challenges that people face and provide strategies for addressing them.

1. Social anxiety: Many people struggle with social anxiety, which can make it difficult to build and maintain social connections. People with social anxiety may feel anxious and self-conscious in social situations, and may avoid social interactions altogether. To address social anxiety, it's important to seek professional help and consider therapy or medication. It can also be helpful to gradually expose yourself to social situations and practice relaxation techniques such as deep breathing or mindfulness.

2. Depression: Depression is a common mental health condition that can make it challenging to engage in social activities and maintain social connections. To address depression, it's important to seek professional help and consider therapy or medication. Engaging in physical

activity, practicing relaxation techniques, and connecting with supportive social connections can also be helpful.

3. Trauma: Trauma can have a significant impact on mental health and can make it difficult to build and maintain social connections. People who have experienced trauma may struggle with trust and may avoid social interactions altogether. To address trauma, it's important to seek professional help and consider therapy or other specialized treatments such as cognitive processing therapy. It's also important to find supportive social connections who can provide a safe and validating environment.

4. Grief and loss: Grief and loss are common experiences that can impact mental health and social connections. People who are grieving may feel isolated and may struggle to connect with others. To address grief and loss, it's important to seek professional help and consider therapy or support groups. Connecting with supportive social connections and engaging in self-care activities can also be helpful.

Conclusion:

Social connections play a critical role in mental health and can have a positive impact on well-being. By understanding the importance of social connections and addressing common mental health challenges, people can work towards building and maintaining strong social connections that can support their mental health.

How Social Connections Can Help with Mental Health

Social connections have been shown to have a significant impact on mental health. A lack of social support can lead to feelings of loneliness, isolation, and low self-esteem, which can increase the risk of developing mental health disorders. On the other hand, strong social connections can provide a sense of belonging, reduce stress, and increase feelings of happiness and well-being.

One way in which social connections can help with mental health is through emotional support. Having people in one's life who can provide emotional support during difficult times can help to reduce the negative impact of stress and improve coping abilities. Emotional support can come in many forms, such as offering a listening ear, providing reassurance and encouragement, or simply being there for someone when they need it most.

Social connections can also help to improve mental health by providing a sense of belonging and community. Feeling like one is a part of a group or community can help to reduce feelings of loneliness and isolation. Being a part of a community can also provide opportunities for social engagement, which can be beneficial for mental health. Participating in group activities, such as sports teams, book clubs, or volunteer organizations, can help to promote a sense of belonging and improve overall well-being.

In addition to emotional support and a sense of belonging, social connections can also help to improve mental health by providing a sense of purpose and meaning. When individuals feel connected to others and engaged in their community, they are more likely to feel that their life has meaning and purpose. This can be especially important for individuals who are struggling with mental health challenges, as having a sense of purpose can provide motivation and a reason to continue to move forward.

Overall, social connections are crucial for maintaining good mental health. They provide emotional support, a sense of belonging, and purpose and meaning in life. By investing in and nurturing social connections, individuals can improve their mental health and overall well-being.

Chapter 5: Comparing and Contrasting Methods
Summary of Pros and Cons

In the previous chapters, we discussed the different types of social connections, the latest technology for staying connected, tips for building and maintaining social connections, and the relationship between social connections and mental health. In this chapter, we will compare and contrast the various methods of building and maintaining social connections and summarize their pros and cons.

Face-to-Face Interactions:

One of the most traditional and effective ways to build and maintain social connections is through face-to-face interactions. Meeting with others in person allows for more genuine and meaningful conversations, and can lead to the formation of deeper relationships. The ability to read body language and non-verbal cues can also enhance the quality of communication and understanding.

Pros:

- More genuine and meaningful conversations

- Leads to deeper relationships

- Better communication through body language and non-verbal cues

Cons:

- May be difficult to schedule and coordinate meeting times

- May not be possible if individuals are geographically separated

- Can be affected by personal insecurities or shyness

Technology-Based Interactions:

In the digital age, technology has made it easier to stay connected with others even when they are not physically present. Social media, video conferencing, and messaging apps are just a few examples of the many ways that people can communicate with each other from anywhere in the world.

Pros:

- Convenient and easy to use

- Allows for communication with people who are geographically distant

- Can be helpful for people who are shy or socially anxious

Cons:

- May be less genuine or meaningful compared to face-to-face interactions

- Can be overwhelming or distracting due to constant notifications and updates

- May contribute to feelings of loneliness or isolation if used excessively

Group Activities:

Participating in group activities, such as sports teams or hobby groups, is another effective way to build and maintain social connections. Group activities provide a shared interest or goal that can bring people together and help them form friendships.

Pros:

- Provides a shared interest or goal
- Helps build a sense of community and belonging
- Can lead to long-lasting friendships

Cons:

- May require a significant time commitment
- May be difficult to find a group with similar interests
- May not be possible for individuals with limited mobility or access to transportation

Volunteering:

Volunteering is another way to build and maintain social connections while also giving back to the community. Volunteering can provide a sense of purpose and fulfillment, while also allowing individuals to meet like-minded people who share a common goal.

Pros:

- Provides a sense of purpose and fulfillment

- Can lead to meaningful connections with others who share a common goal

- Contributes to the community and helps others

Cons:

- May require a significant time commitment

- May not be possible for individuals with limited mobility or physical ability

- May not be possible for individuals who work long hours or have other time constraints

In conclusion, there are many methods of building and maintaining social connections, each with its own set of pros and cons. While face-to-face interactions may provide the most genuine and meaningful connections, technology-based interactions can be convenient for those who are geographically distant or have social anxiety. Group activities and volunteering provide a sense of community and shared interests, while also contributing to the greater good. Ultimately, the best method for building and maintaining social connections will depend on individual preferences and circumstances, and a combination of methods may be the most effective approach.

Criteria for Comparison

In this chapter, we will compare and contrast the different methods of building and maintaining social connections that we have discussed throughout the book. While each method has its unique benefits and drawbacks, certain criteria can be used to evaluate them and determine which method may be most effective for a particular individual.

1. Convenience

One criterion to consider is the convenience of the method. Some methods, such as social media and texting, are very convenient as they can be done from anywhere and at any time. On the other hand, face-to-face interactions may require more time and effort to plan and carry out, but they may provide a more meaningful and fulfilling experience.

2. Quality of Interaction

Another criterion is the quality of interaction. Face-to-face interactions provide a greater opportunity for nonverbal cues, such as facial expressions and body language, which can enhance the quality of the interaction. On the other hand, online interactions may be more impersonal and lack the richness of face-to-face interactions.

3. Social Skills Development

Another criterion is the development of social skills. Face-to-face interactions provide opportunities for individuals to practice and improve their social skills, such as active listening and effective communication. In contrast, online interactions may not provide the same opportunities for social skills development.

4. Scope of Connections

Another criterion is the scope of connections. Social media and other online methods provide opportunities to connect with a larger number of people, including those who may be geographically distant. In contrast, face-to-face interactions may be limited to a smaller group of people, primarily those who are in close proximity.

5. Emotional Support

Finally, a criterion for comparison is emotional support. Some methods may provide more emotional support than others, depending on the type of interaction. For example, online support groups may provide emotional support for individuals who are dealing with specific issues or challenges, while face-to-face interactions with close friends or family members may provide more personalized and intimate emotional support.

Overall, these criteria can be used to evaluate the different methods of building and maintaining social connections and determine which method may be most effective for a particular individual. It is important to consider personal preferences, lifestyle, and goals when selecting a method for building and maintaining social connections.

Recommendations for Different Needs

While all types of social connections can be beneficial, different needs may require different approaches. In this section, we'll provide recommendations for social connection methods that may be most effective for specific needs.

1. Making New Connections: If you're looking to make new connections, joining social clubs, taking classes, or attending networking events may be the way to go. These opportunities can help you meet new people with shared interests and build relationships over time. Online groups and forums may also be helpful in finding like-minded individuals.

2. Maintaining Existing Connections: If you already have a strong social network but struggle to maintain those connections due to a busy schedule or distance, utilizing technology can be a great option. Video calls and social media can help keep you in touch with those you care about, no matter where you are.

3. Coping with Mental Health Challenges: If you're struggling with mental health challenges, seeking professional help is always recommended. However, building and maintaining social connections can also be an effective part of a mental health support system. Joining support groups or attending therapy groups can provide a safe and

supportive environment to connect with others who are going through similar experiences.

4. Combating Loneliness: If you're feeling lonely and isolated, it's important to reach out to others and build new connections. Joining social clubs, volunteering, or attending community events can be great ways to meet new people and build relationships. Additionally, utilizing technology to stay in touch with friends and family can help combat feelings of loneliness.

5. Nurturing Close Relationships: If you're looking to strengthen your close relationships, setting aside time for meaningful activities together can be helpful. This could include taking a trip together, trying a new hobby, or simply spending quality time catching up. Additionally, expressing gratitude and offering support and encouragement can help maintain strong relationships.

Overall, it's important to assess your own needs and choose social connection methods that will work best for you. Whether it's making new connections, maintaining existing ones, or coping with mental health challenges, there are many options available to help you build and strengthen your social support system.

Conclusion
Recap of Importance of Maintaining Social Connections

In conclusion, this book has explored the many benefits of social connections, the latest technology for staying connected, tips and tricks for building and maintaining connections, and the importance of social connections for mental health. Throughout this book, it has become clear that social connections are a crucial aspect of a happy and healthy life.

To recap, the importance of maintaining social connections cannot be overstated. Studies have shown that people who have strong social connections have a lower risk of developing a range of health problems, including cardiovascular disease, depression, and anxiety. Social connections can also improve our immune system, helping us to fight off illness and disease.

Furthermore, staying connected with others can help us to feel more supported and less isolated, which can be especially important during difficult times. When we feel connected to others, we are more likely to seek help when we need it, which can lead to better outcomes for our mental health.

In today's world, there are many different ways to stay connected, from social media platforms to video chat apps. However, it's important to use these technologies wisely and to not let them replace face-to-face connections. Building and maintaining social connections takes effort, but the benefits are well worth it.

In summary, this book has highlighted the many benefits of social connections, the latest technology for staying connected, tips and tricks for building and maintaining connections, and the importance of social connections for mental health. By prioritizing our social connections, we can lead happier, healthier, and more fulfilling lives.

Final Thoughts and Recommendations

In conclusion, the importance of maintaining social connections cannot be overstated. From the benefits of physical health and emotional wellbeing to the role of social connections in building resiliency and addressing mental health challenges, the evidence is clear that connections with others are essential to our overall quality of life.

As we have seen throughout this book, there are many types of social connections and a range of methods for building and maintaining them. Whether through face-to-face interactions, digital communication, or shared hobbies and interests, there is no one-size-fits-all approach to connecting with others. It is up to each individual to determine what works best for their needs and circumstances.

However, while technology has made it easier than ever to stay connected, it is important to remain aware of the potential downsides and to use these tools mindfully. Balancing the convenience and efficiency of digital communication with the benefits of in-person interaction can be a key factor in maintaining healthy social connections.

In terms of recommendations, it is important to prioritize quality over quantity in social connections. While having a large number of connections can be beneficial, the strength and depth of those connections are what truly matter. Additionally, seeking out opportunities to connect with others who share similar interests and values can help to deepen those connections and provide a sense of community and belonging.

Ultimately, the key to building and maintaining social connections is to remain open, authentic, and proactive. This can mean stepping out of your comfort zone to meet new people, making time for regular social activities, and maintaining ongoing communication with those who are important to you.

In a world that is increasingly complex and fast-paced, social connections remain a critical component of our overall wellbeing. By prioritizing these connections and taking proactive steps to build and maintain them, we can lead healthier, happier, and more fulfilling lives.

THE END

Potential References

Introduction:

Holt-Lunstad, J., Smith, T. B., & Layton, J. B. (2010). Social relationships and mortality risk: A meta-analytic review. PLoS medicine, 7(7), e1000316. doi: 10.1371/journal.pmed.1000316

Cacioppo, J. T., & Patrick, W. (2008). Loneliness: Human nature and the need for social connection. WW Norton & Company.

Chapter 1: Types of Social Connections

Umberson, D., & Montez, J. K. (2010). Social relationships and health: A flashpoint for health policy. Journal of health and social behavior, 51(Suppl), S54-S66. doi: 10.1177/0022146510383501

House, J. S., Landis, K. R., & Umberson, D. (1988). Social relationships and health. Science, 241(4865), 540-545. doi: 10.1126/science.3399889

Chapter 2: Technology for Social Connections

Verduyn, P., Ybarra, O., Résibois, M., Jonides, J., & Kross, E. (2017). Do social network sites enhance or undermine subjective well-being? A critical review. Social Issues and Policy Review, 11(1), 274-302. doi: 10.1111/sipr.12033

Burke, M., & Kraut, R. (2016). The relationship between Facebook use and well-being depends on communication type and tie strength. Journal of Computer-Mediated Communication, 21(4), 265-281. doi: 10.1111/jcc4.12162

Chapter 3: Building and Maintaining Social Connections

Lee, R. M., & Robbins, S. B. (1998). The relationship between social connectedness and anxiety, self-esteem, and social identity. Journal of Counseling Psychology, 45(3), 338-345. doi: 10.1037/0022-0167.45.3.338

Cornwell, B. (2011). The dynamic properties of social support: Decay, growth, and staticity, and their effects on adolescent depression. Social Science & Medicine, 73(4), 576-583. doi: 10.1016/j.socscimed.2011.05.032

Chapter 4: Social Connections and Mental Health

Cacioppo, J. T., & Hawkley, L. C. (2009). Perceived social isolation and cognition. Trends in Cognitive Sciences, 13(10), 447-454. doi: 10.1016/j.tics.2009.06.005

Holt-Lunstad, J., Smith, T. B., Baker, M., Harris, T., & Stephenson, D. (2015). Loneliness and social isolation as risk factors for mortality: A meta-analytic review. Perspectives on Psychological Science, 10(2), 227-237. doi: 10.1177/1745691614568352

Chapter 5: Comparing and Contrasting Methods

Martínez-Pérez, B., de la Torre-Díez, I., & López-Coronado, M. (2015). Mobile health applications for the most prevalent conditions by the World Health Organization: Review and analysis. Journal of Medical Internet Research,

Eysenbach, G. (2005). The law of attrition. Journal of medical Internet research, 7(1), e11. doi: 10.2196/jmir.7.1.e11

Hampton, K. N., Goulet, L. S., Rainie, L., & Purcell, K. (2011). Social networking sites and our lives. Pew Research Center.

Kalpidou, M., Costin, D., & Morris, J. (2011). The relationship between Facebook and the well-being of undergraduate college students. Cyberpsychology, Behavior, and Social Networking, 14(4), 183-189. doi: 10.1089/cyber.2010.0061

Lin, N., Dean, A., & Ensel, W. M. (1986). Social support, life events, and depression. Academic Press.

Morgan, A. J., Jorm, A. F., & Mackinnon, A. J. (2013). Internet-based recruitment to a depression prevention intervention: Lessons from the Mood Memos study. Journal of medical Internet research, 15(2), e31. doi: 10.2196/jmir.2308

Nair, U. S., & Chalmers, M. (2018). Designing social media to support social connectedness in older adults. Gerontechnology, 17(1), 1-11. doi: 10.4017/gt.2018.17.1.002.00

Orth, U., Robins, R. W., & Roberts, B. W. (2008). Low self-esteem prospectively predicts depression in adolescence and young adulthood. Journal of personality and social psychology, 95(3), 695-708. doi: 10.1037/0022-3514.95.3.695

Pantic, I. (2014). Online social networking and mental health. Cyberpsychology, Behavior, and Social Networking, 17(10), 652-657. doi: 10.1089/cyber.2014.0070

Petty, R. E., & Cacioppo, J. T. (1986). The elaboration likelihood model of persuasion. Advances in Experimental Social Psychology, 19, 123-205. doi: 10.1016/s0065-2601(08)60214-2

Quinlan, D., Swain, N., & Vella-Brodrick, D. (2011). Character strengths interventions: Building on what we know for improved outcomes. Journal of Happiness Studies, 12(5), 949-962. doi: 10.1007/s10902-010-9238-0

Scogin, F., Welsh, D., Hanson, A., Stump, J., & Coates, A. (2005). Evidence-based psychotherapies for depression in older adults. Clinical psychology: Science and practice, 12(3), 222-237. doi: 10.1093/clipsy.bpi027

Song, H., Zmyslinski-Seelig, A., Kim, J., Drent, A. M., Victor, A., Omori, K., & Allen, M. (2014). Does Facebook make you lonely?: A meta analysis. Computers in Human Behavior, 36, 446-452. doi: 10.1016/j.chb.2014.04.011

Conclusion:

Hawkley, L. C., & Cacioppo, J. T. (2010). Loneliness matters: a theoretical and empirical review of consequences and mechanisms. Annals of behavioral medicine, 40(2), 218-227.

House, J. S., Landis, K. R., & Umberson, D. (1988). Social relationships and health. Science, 241(4865), 540-545.

Uchino, B. N. (2006). Social support and health: a review of physiological processes potentially underlying links to disease outcomes. Journal of behavioral medicine, 29(4), 377-387.

Baumeister, R. F., & Leary, M. R. (1995). The need to belong: desire for interpersonal attachments as a fundamental human motivation. Psychological Bulletin, 117(3), 497-529.

Cacioppo, J. T., & Patrick, W. (2008). Loneliness: Human Nature and the Need for Social Connection. New York: W.W. Norton & Co.

Holt-Lunstad, J., Smith, T. B., & Layton, J. B. (2010). Social relationships and mortality risk: a meta-analytic review. PLoS medicine, 7(7), e1000316.

www.ingramcontent.com/pod-product-compliance
Lightning Source LLC
LaVergne TN
LVHW012127070526
838202LV00056B/5907